America at WAR

CIVIL WAR

TEN GREATEST BATTLES

John Perritano

Created by Q2AMedia

www.q2amedia.com

Text, design, and illustrations copyright © 2011 Leopard Learning

Editor Jessica Cohn
Publishing Director Chester Fisher
Client Service Manager Sujatha Menon
Project Manager Kunal Mehrotra
Art Director Joita Das
Designers Gaurav Arora and Rohit Juneja
Picture Researcher Akansha Srivastava

10 9 8 7 6 5 4 3 2 1

ISBN: 978-81-907857-7-8

Printed in China

Picture Credits
t= top, b=bottom, l=left, r=right, c=center

Cover Image: Kurz & Allison/Popular Graphic Arts/Library of Congress, Currier & Ives/Popular Graphic Arts/Library of Congress.

Title Page: Currier & Ives/Popular Graphic Arts/Library of Congress.

Imprint Page: Gardner, Alexander/Civil War Photographs/Library of Congress

4: Mathew Brady Collection/DoDmedia; 5t: National Archives and Records Administration; 5b: Currier & Ives/Popular Graphic Arts/Library of Congress; 6: Brady National Photographic Art Gallery/Civil War Photographs/

Library of Congress; 7: Kurz & Allison, Art Publishers,Chicago,U.S.A/Popular Graphic Arts/Library of Congress; 8: Fowx, Edgar Guy/ Civil War Photographs/Library of Congress; 9: L. Prang & Co., Boston/Popular Graphic Arts/ Library of Congress; 10: Gibson, James F/ Civil War Photographs/Library of Congress; 11: Mathew Brady Collection/DoDmedia; 12: Gardner, Alexander/Civil War Photographs/ Library of Congress; 13: Gardner, Alexander/ Civil War Photographs/Library of Congress; 14-15: Kurz&Allison, Art Publishers,Chicago,U.S.A/ Popular Graphic Arts/Library of Congress; 16: Brady-Handy Collection/Library of Congress; 17: Gardner, James, b/Civil War Photographs/ Library of Congress; 18: Mathew Brady Collection/DoDmedia; 19: National Archives and Records Administration; 20: Civil War

Photographs/Library of Congress; 21t: Civil War Photographs/Library of Congress; 21b: Civil War Photographs/Library of Congress; 22: A. Gardner/Library of Congress; 23: Gardner, Alexander/Civil War Photographs/Library of Congress; 24: Detroit Publishing Company Photograph Collection/Library of Congress; 25: Photolibrary; 26: David Knox/DoDmedia; 27: O'Sullivan, Timothy H/Civil War Photographs/ Library of Congress; 28: O'Sullivan, Timothy H/ Civil War Photographs/Library of Congress; 29: Civil War Photographs/Library of Congress; 31: Barnard,George N/Civil War Photographs/Library of Congress.

Q2AMedia Art Bank: 7, 9, 11, 13, 15, 19, 23, 25, 29, 30.

Contents

April Morning

The first shots of the American Civil War were fired in the early morning of April 12, 1861. The fighting broke out in Charleston, South Carolina.

In early 1861, South Carolina and several other Southern states **seceded** from the United States and formed the Confederate States of America. Many leaders in the South feared that Abraham Lincoln, the newly elected president of the United States, would abolish **slavery**. Slaves provided labor on the farms, and farming was the South's biggest business.

On April 12, Major Robert Anderson was in command of the U.S. Army forces stationed at Fort Sumter, a small island fortress in Charleston Harbor. For months, Confederate troops had been positioning heavy guns around the fort. Their goal was to stop **Federal** ships from supplying Anderson's troops.

Abraham Lincoln, the sixteenth U.S. president, opposed slavery.

Guns Ablaze

At 4:30 A.M., Confederate Brigadier General P.G.T. Beauregard gave the order to fire on Fort Sumter. The citizens of Charleston watched the 34-hour bombardment. Outgunned and outnumbered, Anderson was forced to surrender the fort.

Only one soldier died in the first battle of the Civil War—a Confederate who was injured when a cannon misfired. But by the time the war ended four years later, the Confederacy would lie in ruins, and more than 600,000 Americans from both sides would be dead. Their bodies would litter some of the bloodiest battlefields in history.

Brigadier General P.G.T. Beauregard gave the order to fire the first shots of the Civil War.

Fort Sumter was the target of intensive shelling by the Confederacy.

Bull Run and Manassas ★ 1

Three months after the war started, General Beauregard, the hero of Fort Sumter, marched north with Confederate troops. Union Brigadier General Irvin McDowell advanced into northeastern Virginia. The two sides met at a creek near the Confederacy's capital.

McDowell's goal was to capture a rail line that ran to Richmond, Virginia, the capital of the Confederacy. Residents of Washington, D.C., the Union's capital, packed picnic lunches and rode buggies to see the battle unfold.

It began more like a carnival than a war. McDowell's troops had never been in battle before. As they marched into Virginia, they broke ranks and picked berries. They left much of their heavy equipment on the side of the road.

Brigadier General Irvin McDowell lost the first major battle of the war at a creek called Bull Run.

Plan of Attack

Federal Army:	Brigadier General Irvin McDowell
Confederacy:	Brigadier General P.G.T. Beauregard, Brigadier General Joseph E. Johnston
Tactics:	Control a strategic railroad junction
Where:	Manassas, Virginia
When:	July 21, 1861

At Bull Run, Rebel forces overran Union troops.

"Stonewall" Jackson

Beauregard was outnumbered. But he placed his troops in an eight-mile line along the southern bank of a creek called Bull Run, near Manassas. The fighting broke out on July 21, 1861.

McDowell attacked the Confederates' left **flank**, battling at a place known as Sudley Springs Ford. The Union general also attacked the center of the line at a place called Stone Bridge. The center attack was a **diversion** to draw Rebel troops away from the left.

The Rebels began to retreat. Then, Confederate Brigadier General Joseph E. Johnston arrived with **reinforcements**. A group of Virginians under the command of Brigadier General Thomas J. Jackson mounted a strong defense. In the thick of the battle, one Rebel general shouted to his troops: "There stands Jackson like a stone wall! Rally behind the Virginians!" The Confederate lines held, and Jackson earned the nickname "Stonewall."

The Great Skedaddle

By mid-afternoon, the Rebels had regrouped. They overran the Union lines. The Federals returned to Washington, D.C., in a retreat that was called the "Great Skedaddle." The Union defeat shook up the North. Before the battle, many Northerners believed the war would end quickly with an easy Northern victory. After the fighting, it appeared that both sides were in for a long slog. The battle was called the First Battle of Bull Run in the North. In the South, it was known as the First Battle of Manassas. It left 4,500 troops on both sides killed, wounded, or captured.

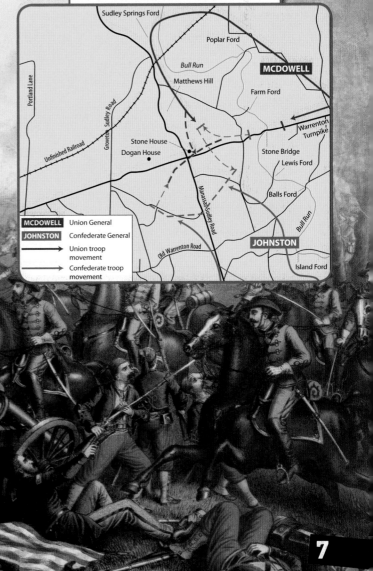

First Battle of Bull Run
First Battle of Manassas

Sudley Springs Ford
Poplar Ford
Bull Run
MCDOWELL
Matthews Hill
Farm Ford
Portland Lane
Groveton Sudley Road
Warrenton Turnpike
Unfinished Railroad
Stone House
Dogan House
Stone Bridge
Lewis Ford
Manassas Sudley Road
Balls Ford
Bull Run
MCDOWELL — Union General
JOHNSTON — Confederate General
→ Union troop movement
→ Confederate troop movement
Old Warrenton Road
JOHNSTON
Island Ford

The Battle of Shiloh

By the spring of 1862, U.S. Major General Ulysses S. Grant had scored victories against the Confederates at Fort Henry, on the Tennessee River, and at Fort Donelson, on the Cumberland River.

Grant and nearly 44,000 Union troops were camped on the west side of the Tennessee River during the first week of April. They waited to link up with Union General Don Carlos Buell and the Army of the Ohio. Their plan was to join forces and march deep into Mississippi.

Time to Advance

Confederate General Albert Sidney Johnston planned to attack before Buell reached Grant. On the morning of April 6, the Confederates opened fire and charged into the Union camp, surprising the Federals. Grant was not expecting an attack. On the first day of battle, he was at his headquarters, nine miles away.

Plan of Attack

Federal Army: Major General Ulysses S. Grant
Confederacy: General Albert Sidney Johnston
Tactics: Drive the enemy out of Tennessee
Where: Shiloh Church, Tennessee
When: April 6–7, 1862

Ulysses S. Grant was a failed shopkeeper, but a brilliant general.

Sunken Road

Fighting began on a hill near a church named Shiloh. The Rebels rushed up the hill as Yankee soldiers fell back. But the center of the Federal line held. Union troops hid behind thick brush that grew along a sunken road near the church. Wave after wave of Confederates tried to force the Yankees from that position. The site became known as the "Hornets' Nest."

The Peach Orchard

To the left of the Hornets' Nest was a peach orchard filled with Union troops. The Confederates sent charge after charge to take out the Union soldiers. At last, the Union line broke, but the Confederates paid a price. General Johnston was severely wounded. He died that afternoon.

The Battle of Shiloh was considered a Union victory, but the Confederates lost fewer soldiers.

Buell Arrives

Fighting began again the next day. Buell arrived with 25,000 fresh Union troops. At dawn, Grant counterattacked and regained the ground lost the day before. By evening, the Confederates had withdrawn.

More than 100,000 troops fought at Shiloh. More than 23,000 were wounded, killed, or missing. The Battle of Shiloh transformed the Union Army of the West into a powerful fighting force.

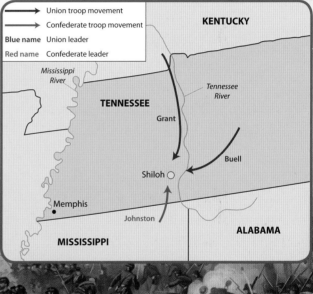

Battle of Shiloh

→ Union troop movement
→ Confederate troop movement
Blue name Union leader
Red name Confederate leader

KENTUCKY

Mississippi River

Tennessee River

TENNESSEE

Grant

Buell

Shiloh ○

Memphis

Johnston

ALABAMA

MISSISSIPPI

Peninsula Campaign ⭐③

President Lincoln chose Major General George B. McClellan to lead the Union army in the east. Nicknamed "Little Mac" by his men, McClellan whipped the Army of the Potomac into shape. Unfortunately for the Union, that's about all the general did.

McClellan's army vastly outnumbered the nearest Confederate army. Yet, for weeks McClellan refused to leave Washington. Under pressure by an impatient president and other political leaders, McClellan finally left camp and advanced toward the Confederate capital.

"I will bring you now face to face with the rebels," he told his men.

The North's mighty factories produced its many weapons.

Plan of Attack

Federal Army:	Major General George B. McClellan
Confederacy:	General Robert E. Lee
Tactics:	Capture Richmond
Where:	Virginia
Date:	April–July 1862

Crawling to Richmond

McClellan left Washington and headed toward Richmond on March 17, 1862. Boats ferried 121,500 troops down the Potomac River to the York-James Peninsula. From there, the Union army slogged westward.

The campaign did not begin well. McClellan spent a month in a **siege** of Yorktown, which proved to be unnecessary. The Rebels used this delay to reinforce Richmond. They knew an all-out Federal assault was coming.

Lee Takes Command

Leaving Yorktown, McClellan moved at a snail-like pace toward Richmond. He came within five miles of the capital on May 31. He did not get much farther. The task of defending the South's capital had fallen to Confederate General Robert E. Lee, and Lee drove McClellan away. The Peninsula Campaign showed both McClellan's weakness and Lee's brilliance as a commander. The Confederate general began planning a bold invasion of the North.

Battles of the Peninsula Campaign

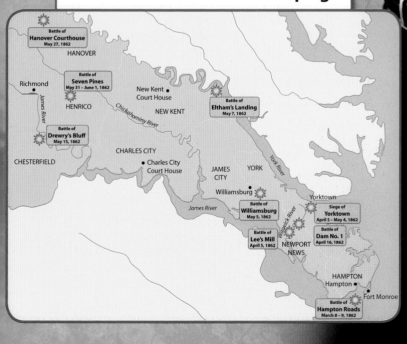

Major General George McClellan's nickname was "Little Napoleon."

Antietam

On September 13, 1862, Union soldiers found a lost package in a meadow near Frederick, Maryland. The bulky envelope held three cigars. Wrapped around the cigars was a copy of General Lee's battle plans.

President Lincoln visited the Antietam battlefield soon after the fighting was over.

Plan of Attack

Federal Army:	Major General George B. McClellan
Confederacy:	General Robert E. Lee
Tactics:	Invasion of the North
Where:	Antietam Creek, Maryland
When:	September 17, 1862

Lee's Army of Northern Virginia had crossed the Potomac River into Maryland. The Southern general held hopes that the citizens of Maryland—a state on the North-South border—would rally to the Confederate cause. Lee also hoped that a victory on Northern soil would persuade Great Britain to recognize and support Confederate independence. Lee's plan was risky. His army would be fighting far from its food sources and other supplies.

Bloody Lane

Despite having seen Lee's battle plans, Union Major General George McClellan did nothing for two days. During that time, Lee moved his troops. The two armies finally faced off near Antietam Creek, outside of Sharpsburg, Maryland. The battle began on the morning of September 17.

Brigadier General "Stonewall" Jackson led the Confederates into battle. Union troops advanced into the Confederate lines by attacking near a church and cornfield. But the Rebels held together and streamed back across the field. The Union then smashed through the Rebel center at a sunken farm road now known as Bloody Lane. At that moment, McClellan had a chance to defeat Lee's army. Instead the Union general hesitated. The battle then shifted south to a stone bridge.

America's Bloodiest Day

Although McClellan lost more men than Lee, the Union won the battle. Lee retreated across the Potomac River and returned to Virginia. This pleased Abraham Lincoln, who had been looking for a Union victory that would allow him to free the slaves. "God bless you and all with you," the president wired McClellan after learning of the victory. "Destroy the rebel army if possible." McClellan did not, however, pursue the retreating Rebels.

More than 6,000 Americans on both sides died that day, with about 23,000 total casualties (dead, wounded, captured, or missing). It was one of the bloodiest days in U.S. history. Lincoln was able, however, to use this Union "victory" to convince the public to support **emancipation**.

Battle of Antietam

Potomac River
Hooker
Mansfield
Franklin
Stuart
East Wood
West Wood
cornfield
Sumner
Hood
Dunker Church
Jackson
MCCLELLAN
Sunken Road
Hagerstown Turnpike
D.H. Hill
Porter
Sharpsburg
Antietam Creek
LEE
Longstreet
Burnside
A.P. Hill

MCCLELLAN	Union General
LEE	Confederate General
→	Union troop movement
→	Confederate troop movement
Blue name	Union leader
Red name	Confederate leader

The Antietam battlefield was filled with the dead when the fighting ended.

Fredericksburg ★

McClellan's inability to destroy Lee's army angered Lincoln. "He has got the slows," the president said. In November 1862, Lincoln replaced McClellan with Major General Ambrose E. Burnside.

Upon taking command of the Army of the Potomac, Burnside quickly went into action. He marched his army toward Fredericksburg, Virginia, which is on the Rappahannock River, between Richmond and Washington, D.C.

Burnside hoped to capture Fredericksburg and the hills overlooking the town before Lee had a chance to react. However, Burnside needed to build **pontoon** bridges to move his army of nearly 120,000 men across the Rappahannock. It took 17 days to get the bridges in place. This left Lee enough time to place 75,000 troops along the hills above the town.

To fight at Fredericksburg, Union soldiers crossed the Rappahannock River on floating bridges.

Slow Going

On December 11, the Federals began shelling Fredericksburg. The bombs set much of the town on fire. Burnside's men then began crossing the bridges. A **brigade** of Mississippi **sharpshooters** took aim at the Federals. This slowed the advance, but by the next day, all of Burnside's troops had crossed the river.

Plan of Attack

Federal Army:	Major General Ambrose E. Burnside
Confederacy:	General Robert E. Lee
Tactics:	Capture Fredericksburg
Where:	Fredericksburg, Virginia
When:	December 11–15, 1862

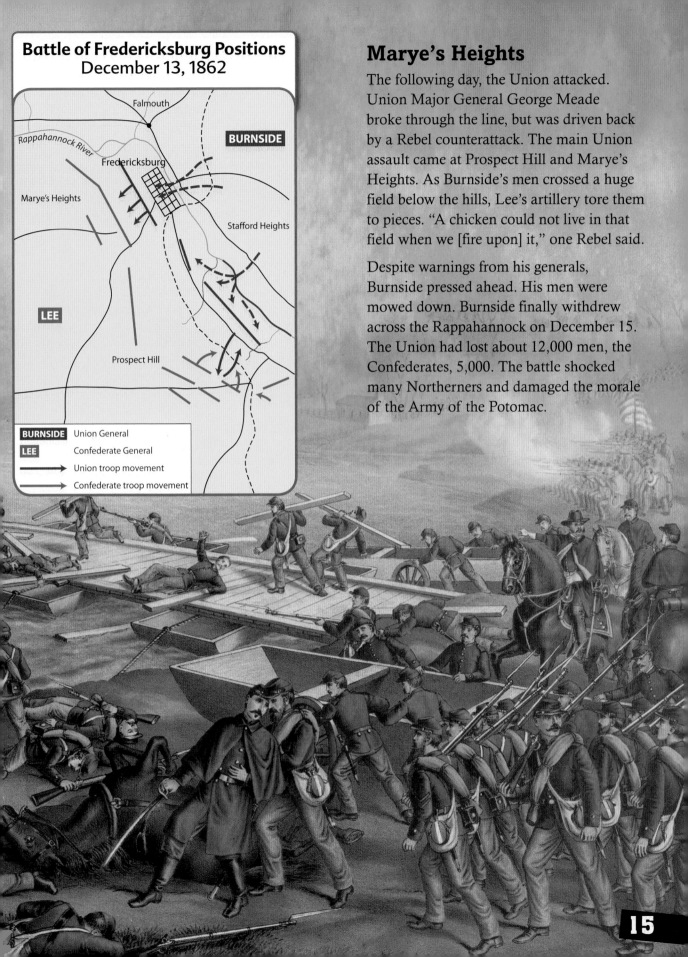

Battle of Fredericksburg Positions
December 13, 1862

Falmouth

Rappahannock River

BURNSIDE

Fredericksburg

Marye's Heights

Stafford Heights

LEE

Prospect Hill

BURNSIDE	Union General
LEE	Confederate General
→	Union troop movement
→	Confederate troop movement

Marye's Heights

The following day, the Union attacked. Union Major General George Meade broke through the line, but was driven back by a Rebel counterattack. The main Union assault came at Prospect Hill and Marye's Heights. As Burnside's men crossed a huge field below the hills, Lee's artillery tore them to pieces. "A chicken could not live in that field when we [fire upon] it," one Rebel said.

Despite warnings from his generals, Burnside pressed ahead. His men were mowed down. Burnside finally withdrew across the Rappahannock on December 15. The Union had lost about 12,000 men, the Confederates, 5,000. The battle shocked many Northerners and damaged the morale of the Army of the Potomac.

Battle of Chancellorsville

In early 1863, the Army of the Potomac was failing. Its loss at Fredericksburg was devastating. Soldiers had not been paid in months and had little to eat. President Lincoln had yet to find a general who could defeat Robert E. Lee.

In January, Lincoln fired Burnside and replaced him with Major General Joseph B. Hooker. With the arrival of spring, Hooker came up with a plan to destroy the Army of Northern Virginia.

The first part of Hooker's **strategy** involved Union Major General John Sedgwick, who would take troops to fight against Lee again at Fredericksburg. Hooker was betting that Lee would defend the town with all his might. Hooker would then cross the Rappahannock and attack the Rebels from the rear, while Lee was fighting Sedgwick. The North would then move against Richmond. "My plans are perfect," Hooker said. "May God have mercy on General Lee, for I will have none."

Union Major General Joseph Hooker devised a plan to destroy the Army of Northern Virginia.

Plan of Attack

Federal Army:	Major General Joseph B. Hooker
Confederacy:	General Robert E. Lee, Major General Thomas J. Jackson
Tactics:	Destroy the Army of Northern Virginia
Where:	Chancellorsville, Virginia
When:	April 30–May 6, 1863

The Wilderness

On May 1, Hooker marched south toward the Confederate lines. The woods were so packed with trees that local residents called the area the "Wilderness." The two armies met in a brief firefight that rattled Hooker. He ordered his men to withdraw. The North took a defensive position around Chancellorsville, and Lee's smaller army went on the offensive.

Outnumbered

Next, Hooker marched toward Chancellorsville, 10 miles west of Fredericksburg. Sedgwick moved on Lee, but Lee was not fooled by Hooker's plan. The Confederate general left 10,000 soldiers to defend Fredericksburg, then took the balance of his 60,000-man army to face Hooker.

Wounded soldiers rested after the Battle of Chancellorsville.

Chancellorsville

On May 2, 1863, Jackson and 26,000 Rebel soldiers marched 14 miles to attack the Union's right flank. Hooker mistakenly believed that Jackson was retreating. As Union soldiers played cards and drank coffee in the early evening, a herd of deer came bounding through the Yankee camp. Behind the animals charged Jackson's men.

The Union soldiers were forced to retreat for two miles. Nightfall finally slowed the Rebel advance. The troops were just short of Chancellorsville. Jackson was a major general by then. He and several Southern officers rode out to look for a place from which they could launch a night attack. As he returned to the Confederate lines, Jackson was mistakenly shot by his own men. The wounded general was taken to a field hospital, where his left arm was **amputated**.

Confederate Major General "Stonewall" Jackson was trained at West Point.

Two Fronts

Confederate Major General J.E.B. Stuart took over for Jackson. On May 3, the battle exploded on two fronts. Stuart launched an attack at dawn, driving the Federals out of Chancellorsville. Meanwhile, Sedgwick's Union forces advanced on Fredericksburg. The Yankees swarmed the hills above the town and attacked the rear of the Confederate army.

Wounded troops awaited help after the Battle of Chancellorsville.

Lee Wins

Lee turned his troops to face the Federals. By May 6, the Union had lost the battle. The Federals retreated across the Rappahannock. The Union had suffered about 17,000 casualties. Victory came at a price for the Rebels as well. About 13,000 Confederates had died—including Stonewall Jackson. Chancellorsville was in many ways Lee's greatest victory. Yet, the Army of the Potomac had escaped, and Lee had lost one of his best generals.

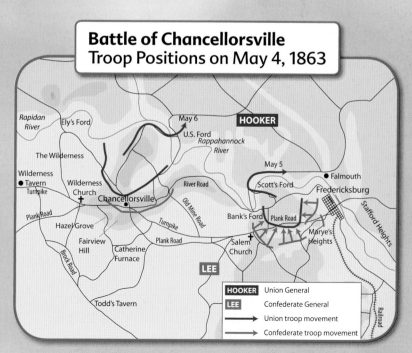

Battle of Chancellorsville
Troop Positions on May 4, 1863

HOOKER	Union General
LEE	Confederate General
→	Union troop movement
→	Confederate troop movement

Battle of Gettysburg

7

Lee's success at Chancellorsville gave the Confederacy new hope. Lee thought that a new invasion of the North would turn public opinion against the war and force President Lincoln to seek peace. The Confederate general marched his troops from Virginia into Pennsylvania.

Officers of the 50th Regiment of the Pennsylvania infantry posed for a picture.

Plan of Attack

Federal Army: Major General George G. Meade

Confederacy: General Robert E. Lee

Tactics: Invade the North

Where: Gettysburg, Pennsylvania

When: July 1–3, 1863

On July 1, 1863, rumors spread that there were shoes for the taking in nearby Gettysburg. The Rebels had been marching a long time and needed new footwear. They **converged** on Gettysburg from the north. But Union **cavalry** spotted them about three miles west of town and started a fight. After a day-long battle, the Rebels chased the outnumbered Yankees through Gettysburg.

Taking the High Ground

Union Major General Winfield Scott Hancock appeared on the scene. He rallied the retreating troops and formed defensive positions on the nearby Culp's Hill and Cemetery Hill. Lee arrived late in the afternoon. He asked Confederate Lieutenant General Richard S. Ewell to take the hills before nightfall if possible. But Ewell did not attack. His inaction allowed Union forces to take the high ground south of town.

The Fish Hook

By nightfall, Federal reinforcements arrived at Gettysburg, and Lee lost his advantage. The Union's front line was shaped like a fishhook. The curve of the hook ran along Culp's Hill. The **shank** snaked across Cemetery Ridge to two hills called Big and Little Round Top. Confederate Lieutenant General James Longstreet advised Lee to move out of Gettysburg and march on Washington. But Lee refused. "The enemy is there," Lee said, "and I'm going to fight him there."

General Robert E. Lee commanded his troops in Gettysburg from this house.

Tents lined the battlefield at Gettysburg from Cemetery Ridge to Little Round Top.

Gettysburg

When morning broke on July 2, 1863, thousands of Confederate and Union troops faced off. Lee wanted to force the Yankees off the high ground. Union Major General George G. Meade was determined to stay.

The Confederates numbered about 70,000. The Union had about 95,000 troops. On the second day of battle, North and South fought on several important spots, including the Peach Orchard, Devil's Den, Cemetery Hill, and a farm named the Wheat Field. Each **skirmish** was a battle within the larger battle. Fighting was so deadly that a small stream near Devil's Den ran red with blood.

The fighting for Little Round Top was especially brutal. Lee knew that if he captured the top of that hill, his men could train their cannons on the Federal line and blow it to pieces. If that happened, the Rebels could win the battle. The Confederates charged up the hill several times. Each time the Union soldiers fought back. With ammunition running low, Union soldiers fixed **bayonets** on their muskets and charged down the hillside. The surprised Confederates fled.

When the fighting ended, Gettysburg was littered with thousands of corpses.

This Confederate soldier fell dead at Devil's Den.

Gettysburg Lines of Battle
July 3, 1863

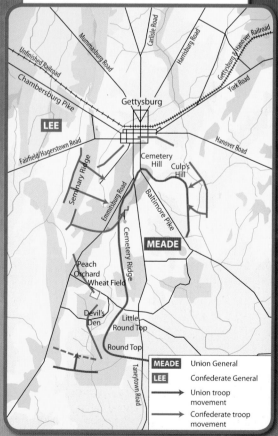

"It Was All My Fault"

By July 3, Lee had not gained any ground. He decided to attack the center of the Federal defense on Cemetery Ridge. Thirteen thousand Confederates under the command of Major General George Pickett bravely advanced into Union fire. Pickett's charge failed. The Confederates were too tired to charge again. Over the three-day battle, about 51,000 troops were killed, wounded, or missing. Gettysburg was the bloodiest battle of the war. It would also be the last time the South would threaten the North on its own soil.

Siege of Vicksburg

8

July 4, 1863, was a good day for President Lincoln. His troops had defeated Lee at Gettysburg the previous day, and Federal forces under Ulysses S. Grant captured Vicksburg, Mississippi, after a 47-day siege.

The Mississippi River was vital to the Confederacy. The river allowed the Confederacy to move troops, cotton, food, and supplies. "Vicksburg is the key," Lincoln said. "The war can never be brought to a close until the key is in our pocket."

A monument was erected to commemorate the surrender of Vicksburg.

Plan of Attack

Federal Army:	Major General Ulysses S. Grant
Confederacy:	Lieutenant General John C. Pemberton
Tactics:	Control the Mississippi River
Where:	Vicksburg, Mississippi
When:	May 18–July 4, 1863

"Dig Our Way In"

The U.S. Navy had failed twice to seize the city. Now, it was Grant's turn. The determined general decided to cross the Mississippi River south of Vicksburg and attack the city from the east. Navy gunboats transported Grant's army across the mile-wide water. Grant then moved swiftly, winning several battles along the way. On May 19, Grant ordered a frontal attack on Vicksburg. The Rebels turned the Yankees away. Grant tried two more assaults. Both failed. "We'll have to dig our way in," Grant said. Union troops began digging a system of ditches from which they could fight.

Laying Siege

Grant positioned some 70,000 troops around Vicksburg. The Union lines formed a semi-circle about seven miles long. Inside the city, Confederate Lieutenant General John C. Pemberton had 30,000 troops, hoping to hold out until help arrived. But Vicksburg was short on food and supplies. Both sides battled day after day in intense heat. Help never arrived. On July 4, Pemberton surrendered. Vicksburg, like Gettysburg, was a turning point. Grant's victory at Vicksburg gave the Union the "key" needed to win the war.

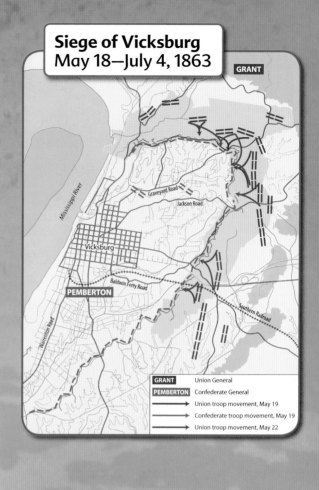

Siege of Vicksburg
May 18—July 4, 1863

GRANT	Union General
PEMBERTON	Confederate General
→	Union troop movement, May 19
→	Confederate troop movement, May 19
→	Union troop movement, May 22

The siege of Vicksburg ended on July 4, 1863.

Battle of the Wilderness

9

In March 1864, President Lincoln placed Grant in charge of all Union armies. With Grant in command, Federal troops worked together. While the Army of the Potomac pursued Lee, Union Brigadier General William T. Sherman fought his way through Georgia to the Atlantic Ocean.

Grant put Major General George G. Meade, the hero of Gettysburg, in charge of the Army of the Potomac. "Wherever Lee goes, about 95,000 you will go also," Grant said.

Lee's strategy now was to turn each battle into a killing field. He hoped the bloodshed finally would turn Northerners against the war and force Lincoln from office during the upcoming election.

Plan of Attack

Federal Army:	Lieutenant General Ulysses S. Grant
Confederacy:	General Robert E. Lee
Tactics:	Destroy the Army of Northern Virginia
Where:	Spotsylvania County, Virginia
When:	May 5–May 7, 1864

At their camps, the Army of the Potomac rested between moves.

Chaos

Grant faced Lee in the two-day Battle of the Wilderness. It would be the first of several battles that would force the South to surrender.

Lee and 60,000 Confederates awaited Grant in the same woods at Chancellorsville that had trapped Hooker and his army in 1863. Fighting began at noon on May 5. The Union attacked the Rebels on the Orange Turnpike. Both sides also battled on the Plank Road. It was chaos. Soldiers fired on their own comrades. The first day of battle ended when darkness fell.

At Port Royal, Virginia, Federal troops loaded a boat with supplies.

Wilderness

On the second day of battle, Union soldiers attacked along the Plank Road, forcing the Rebels to scatter.

Union forces smashed through the center of the Confederate line. But a group of Texans were able to battle the Federals nearby until Confederate Lieutenant General James Longstreet and his troops could arrive.

Federal troops lined the North Anna River in Virginia.

By the end of the second day, about 17,000 Union soldiers had been killed. Brushfires raged across the Wilderness, burning 200 wounded men alive. But Grant pushed forward—something no other Union general had done after a battle. On May 7, the Federals advanced on Spotsylvania Courthouse. Once again, the Yankees and Rebels battled one another to a draw. "General Grant is not going to retreat," Lee told his staff. Lee was right.

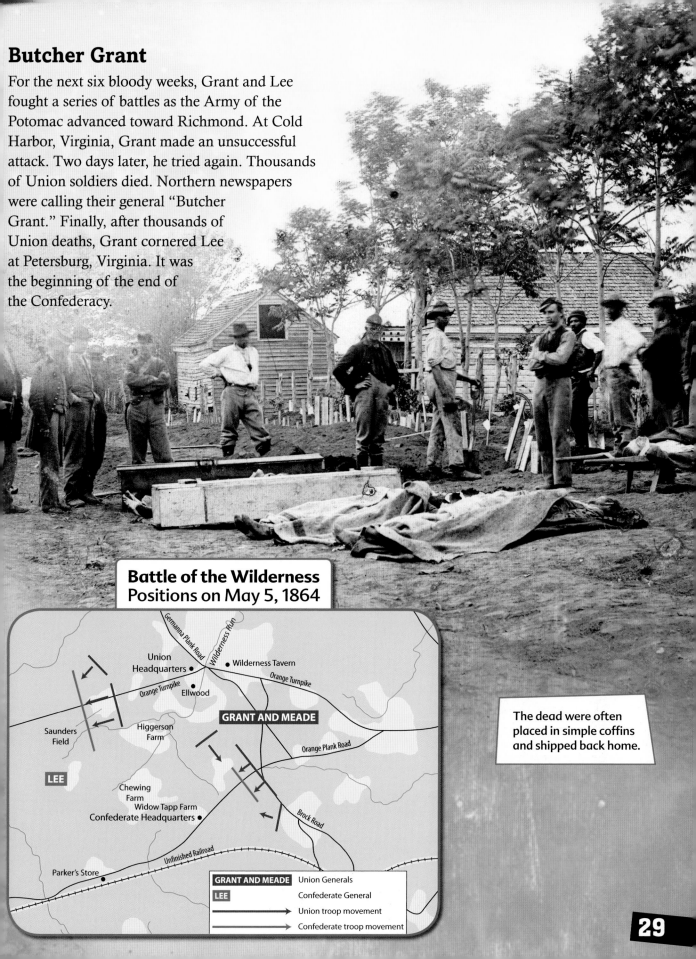

Butcher Grant

For the next six bloody weeks, Grant and Lee fought a series of battles as the Army of the Potomac advanced toward Richmond. At Cold Harbor, Virginia, Grant made an unsuccessful attack. Two days later, he tried again. Thousands of Union soldiers died. Northern newspapers were calling their general "Butcher Grant." Finally, after thousands of Union deaths, Grant cornered Lee at Petersburg, Virginia. It was the beginning of the end of the Confederacy.

Battle of the Wilderness
Positions on May 5, 1864

Germanna Plank Road
Wilderness Run
Union Headquarters
Wilderness Tavern
Orange Turnpike
Orange Turnpike
Ellwood

GRANT AND MEADE

Saunders Field
Higgerson Farm
Orange Plank Road

LEE

Chewing Farm
Widow Tapp Farm
Confederate Headquarters
Brock Road

Unfinished Railroad
Parker's Store

GRANT AND MEADE	Union Generals
LEE	Confederate General
→	Union troop movement
→	Confederate troop movement

The dead were often placed in simple coffins and shipped back home.

March to the Sea

William Tecumseh Sherman was Grant's most trusted officer. The two had survived many hard times together.

As Grant chased Lee through Virginia, Sherman marched to capture Atlanta and smash the Confederate armies led by Joseph E. Johnston. On May 6, 1864, Sherman's Grand Army of the West moved south from Chattanooga, Tennessee, into Georgia.

On the Move

Sherman divided the 98,000 men under his command into three giant columns. Johnston did not have enough men and ammunition to face Sherman head on. He could only hope to slow the Federal advance. One column moved on the right, while another column moved on the left. Still another column marched in the center. Sherman's troops built bridges in order to cross rivers. They ripped up rail lines. The heat was terrible. Yet, Sherman marched on, moving around the Rebel forces.

Johnston was less successful in fighting back. Jefferson Davis, who was president of the Confederacy, replaced Johnston with General John B. Hood.

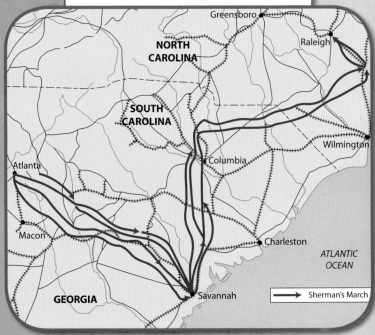

Sherman's Movements November 1864—April 1865

Plan of Attack

Federal Army:	Major General William T. Sherman
Confederacy:	General Joseph E. Johnston, General John B. Hood
Tactics:	Destroy the South's Will to Fight
Where:	Georgia to the Carolinas
When:	November 15–December 21, 1864

In the End

Sherman was made a major general in August. He captured Atlanta early in September 1864. Two months later, Sherman marched to Savannah, Georgia, on the Atlantic coast. Along the way, the Federals destroyed small homes and huge plantations. Sherman's goal was to destroy the Confederacy's will to fight. "The utter destruction of [Georgia's] roads, houses, and people," Sherman wrote, "will cripple their military resources.... I can make Georgia howl!"

Sherman reached Savannah on December 21. He then turned north to the Carolinas. As Sherman marched, Grant continued his campaign in Virginia. Together, they destroyed the Confederacy.

In April 1865, Lee surrendered his army. That same month, Lincoln was assassinated. The last Confederate forces finally surrendered in May. Those who fought in the battles of the Civil War were haunted by the horrors for years to come. The war killed 2 percent of the nation's population. Yet, it also freed 4 million slaves. The dead, Lincoln said, did not "die in vain."

Union troops left Atlanta in ruins as they marched to the sea.

Glossary

amputated—cut off a limb to try to save a life

bayonets—pointed blades that fit on the end of a rifle

brigade—a military unit made up of one or more units of infantry

cavalry—soldiers on horseback

converged—came together

diversion—in war, an attack made to draw the attention of an enemy away from the primary operation

emancipation—freedom from the control of someone else

Federal—belonging to the United States; also known as the "Union" or "North"

flank—the extreme right or left side of an army

pontoon—a floating structure; can serve as a temporary bridge

reinforcements—troops and equipment sent to help

seceded—withdrew

shank—narrow part

sharpshooters—expert marksmen

siege—a military blockade of a fortified place, such as a city

skirmish—short fight

slavery—the buying and selling of human beings for forced labor

strategy—a carefully planned action

Index